Light in Light

Light in Light

Deborah Gerrish

RESOURCE *Publications* • Eugene, Oregon

LIGHT IN LIGHT

Copyright © 2017 Deborah Gerrish. All rights reserved. Except for brief quotations in critical publications or reviews, no part of this book may be reproduced in any manner without prior written permission from the publisher. Write: Permissions, Wipf and Stock Publishers, 199 W. 8th Ave., Suite 3, Eugene, OR 97401.

Resource Publications
An Imprint of Wipf and Stock Publishers
199 W. 8th Ave., Suite 3
Eugene, OR 97401

www.wipfandstock.com

PAPERBACK ISBN: 978-1-5326-1691-4
HARDCOVER ISBN: 978-1-4982-4095-6
EBOOK ISBN: 978-1-4982-4094-9

Manufactured in the U.S.A. JULY 14, 2017

for Jim

Deep in their roots, all flowers keep the light.
—Theodore Roethke

Contents

ONE

    This Morning | 3
    That Winter | 4
    The Return | 6
    First Day of School for the Teacher | 7
    San Diego Afternoon | 8
    The Contest | 9
    Little Women | 11
    Wounded Angel | 12
    The Room | 13
    Winter Garden | 14
    The Deer | 15
    At Dusk | 16
    The Gift | 17
    Paisley Shawl | 18

TWO

    Orange Lantern. Blue Moon Rising | 21
    Portrait in the Trees | 22
    Aroma in Floral | 23
    The Blessing | 24
    Petits Fours | 26
    The Pink Thread | 27
    Bear | 28
    The Visit | 29
    Peeling | 30
    I Turned Around | 31
    Awakenings | 32

Contents

It Was a Day | 33
Seeley's Pond | 34
Evening in July | 35
Olive and Fig | 36
The Anointed Cow | 37

THREE

Messengers | 41
The Easel | 42
At the Beach | 43
Amusement Park | 44
The Cat Undergoes a Breakthrough | 46
After the Squall | 47
The Palace | 48
Odes and Elegies | 49
Delilah | 50
When the Diner Closes | 51
Samson Calls Out | 53
Tree-Whisperer | 54
Flight | 55
I Cry Out to Daddy, Abba | 56
The Storm | 57
The Old Man Looks at the Greenhouse from His Bedroom Window | 58

FOUR

World With No End | 61
She Had a Use for Everything | 62
Under the Beech Tree | 63
Oh, If I Were a Bird and Could Fly Away | 64
Dear White Star Line | 65
Early this Morning | 66
They Be Mortals | 67
The Window | 68
The Liberator | 69
Upon Viewing Masaccio's Carriata dal Paradiso Terrestre | 71
After Ravensbruck: The Woman from Holland Speaks to Me
    in a Dream | 72
I Lift My Eyes | 73

Contents

Eve Looks to the Pear Tree | 74
Memo | 75
Biography of the Pear | 76
Cherry Blossoms | 77
Unlatching | 79

Acknowledgments | 81

Notes | 83

ONE

THIS MORNING

the haze lifted early. In the garden, I planted herbs.
Bluebirds watched. Dew rolled off their feet
like beads of Muscadet.

The woodpecker in search of a mate,
drummed the sycamore tree and I peered
into the flicker's tree cavity,

the small boulevard of insects. Tiny fly-bugs random
against the squint of the sun—
grubs, beetles, termites, frozen in a syrup-sap.

As I listened, I no longer puzzled
over the playlist of the mockingbird.
I no longer remembered winter's

frigid-tin temperature.
I no longer desired to write poems in the cemetery—
near my father's grave.

There was no ache in my bones.
When lifting the planter, I saw the bright
epaulettes of the red winged blackbird.

THAT WINTER

my mother and my father died in February. One that morning
one that evening, four days, one hundred four hours apart. Seasons
later I drive through the old neighborhood past my childhood

friend's brick house with picket fence, our houses back to back.
Years ago I'd babysit his sister on weekend afternoons. Patiently wait
for him in his modern '60s kitchen, as he clicked his bronze toy gun

between bites. A slow-moving, prolonged lunch, one bite at a time,
one click then another. Grilled cheese. Bite, click. With bacon, click,
click. Or peanut butter on toast, click, bite, click. Tried to convince

myself I held no grudge about his caterpillar style. His mother
brushed him along like an autumn fly, pushing swigs of Boscoe
milk to wash the meal down quickly. By mid-afternoon—

we'd take our places outdoors behind rough columns of trees,
play tag beneath the sky with its apricot glow, mortality weighing
on the leaf-spare branches. In the wide back yard, heaps

of maple leaves, stiff azalea and hundreds of acorns. Abandoned
Adirondack chairs, air enriched with pungent smoldering
leaves & wood burning fireplaces. Darting between the willows,

Eric shrieked, *You Jane me Tarzan,* and I chanted, *Eeeee-Ah-Key.*
Giggles & that unforgettable toothy grin from his young sister,
as she chased us in concentric circles between neighbor's yards,

the October air turning crisp like white transparent apples,
the slanted sky against the day's final hour. If only I could
speak to the trees and the shadows of actors.

If only my childhood contained me like the heavenly bodies
protected by stars. I wish I could say I didn't see nightfall
coming or that I wasn't so lost in a retinue of dreams.

I wish I could say I'm not shocked. But I stuff my pillows with lavender flowers so I can sleep through winter.

THE RETURN

The house

on Jefferson Avenue—
1939 mortar, brick, stone
pearly wood shutters

my parents' bedroom window—
crystal leaded glass,
childhood's diamonds.

The door

once sturdy—
painted white
three cape cod windows
brass numbers—
faded and splintered

My kindred

their days dust—
spent
like dried sunflowers.

I roam through rooms,

hear my father's words,
a soft thunder,
my mother calls my name,
calls my name.

FIRST DAY OF SCHOOL FOR THE TEACHER

For Cheryl

    Twenty-first century business suit with
    eyelet white blouse—

    like the red-plaid dress & camel-hair
    coat you couldn't wait to wear

    back in third grade. The marble notebook you
    carried close to your heart. Yellow sharpened
    pencils.

    Mother's apron,
    the bread box, turkey sandwiches wrapped
    in waxed paper. Knee highs, penny loafers. School
    days—

    We are still there. Blue sky
    wider.

SAN DIEGO AFTERNOON

Mission Bay sea lions
somersault over manmade barge—
school's out.

THE CONTEST

His name was Joe—
tall, with curly light brown hair
like my French poodle, Rollo.

He was as cute as the football
captain my younger sister dated,
smarter than my older sister's
college boyfriend.

On Saturdays, we would meet
at the Great Falls just where
the river makes a grand entrance,
creates a brash wall of water.

Cronin's Oak Tree—
two o'clock sharp at Overlook Park,
shared Marlboros like in
Steve McQueen movies—
with every smoke ring, I would flip
my hair back Natalie Wood style.

Dressed in his black bomber jacket
with the red letters, Satan,
stitched across the back,
Joe wore skinny jeans before
they were called skinny jeans.

My dear mother tried
to lure me from this man—

I was the cat and she waved
the wand with bird feathers;
took me shopping,
bought me an angora sweater,

silk stockings and garters,
an organza dress with crinoline,
patent shoes, a chenille beret.

But listen, finally she said, "I forbid you
to see this boy." So we set a time to meet again,
planned to dance at Central High's

First Annual Chubby Checker "Let's Twist Again
Like We Did Last Summer Contest."

My white chiffon dress, red embroidered hem
flared like the trunk on our front yard maple.

We did the twist for hours,
sweating like two unpeeled apples,
our feet sliding, our shoulders and arms
swinging back and forth,
the music loud like the noise of the falls,
my curly long hair out of control.

LITTLE WOMEN

Madame Alexander Dolls displayed in the gleaming
glass windows of Holder's Variety Store. Sisters walk

me to the shop from home to rummage through
blue-floral boxes. Unfolding layers of tissue, we

marvel at dolls & miniature wardrobes of clothes.
Cissy Doll with chestnut hair and cream-rose complexion,

adorned in her coral chiffon hat framed in tulle
roseate trim, the moiré knee-length dress with three

quarter sleeves. On the dressing table, her soft silkaline
fabric brushes my wrists. The ballerina flared A-line

enhances her unblemished figure. That wide-eyed belle,
brilliant eyes with curvy lashes, lids that close and open.

I try on my doll's hat; hold up her dress to the mirror.
Like the magnolia, her silence awakens

a wide sky, a cloud of being. Little women—
heritage creatures of eternity, flawless

porcelain faces, permanent rouge and
chignoned hair, starry eyes, ageless

pouting lips. Perfect. World without end like etched
scenes on an urn: hope & truth & grace in perpetuum.

WOUNDED ANGEL

—after Hugo Simberg's *The Wounded Angel*, 1902, oil painting

There are good angels and bad ones. Some dazzle, others bleed
mischief from their eyes. I speak to the ethereal kind yet not the

evil fallen ones. I'm not talking about cupids scrolled on valentine
cards but the genre Billy Graham writes about. The hedges

of angels above beneath behind and beside. Though we are
a little less than the angels, sometimes injured seraphim and

cherubim need our human help. If you should witness one in your
spirit that crash-lands in a haystack in the meadowlands, dangles

from a city bridge, or gathers snowdrops along the wrong road, carry
the crippled, then lift the briefly powerless to the air again.

It could be a fiery dart pierced its legs in battle or principalities tied
back its wings in flight. Or maybe it flew too close to the sun.

Sometimes in the early dawn, I've heard the chimes of summer,
I've seen an angel rise—
        from where its heels dug dust.

THE ROOM

When I think back to the room where I was born,
I can't help thinking of that other room.

Permanent five o'clock shadow,
eye glasses tight in your dropped right hand.

You in the leather chair, plaid slippers, the unread
NY Times stacked on the nest

of tables, chin on your chest.
The Yankee game drones across airways.

The smell of overcooked lamb chop and onions,
last night's dishes piled in the farmhouse sink—

I unlock the front door; push through each room
imagine my mother, breathing, grunting, screaming—

your brown hat and worn gloves
on the chair in the hallway.

Ben Hogan putter leaning in the corner,
waving at me when I found you.

WINTER GARDEN

It's Thursday. It's snowing. It's
February. I am spending the afternoon
with Czeslaw Milosz.

Through the open door, the chimes of
the city. The earth's chimes.

He is sipping bilberry tea
in my cramped kitchen nook. Slowly,

he recites his poems. On the table,
a vase of sunflowers. Bread and jam.

Through the yard-window—
the wind. A family of deer in single
file walk in each other's steps.

It's Thursday and February and it's snowing,
I am spending the afternoon with Milosz—

THE DEER

At dusk, one appears on the crystal-snow
then another, then two more—
now a constellation outside the window.

The one with ears like butterfly-wings wags its
tail flagging the others: morse code,
stomps and snorts, its white-throat contorted.

Two does spring high rocking back and forth.
Standing out like the north star, the buck
sprints past the house & down the salted-road.

Deer follow single file in his footprints.

What do I know of deer
kindnesses? Fawns, doe & buck,
their urgent glances,

their game of touch, their playfulness.
When the next meal appears & how to forage
through the ice of winter for nuts, twigs and lichens—

how to outwit the coyote in a single bound,
swim faster than the mountain lion.

AT DUSK

I bundle in my sweater

like grave clothes in the cemetery

near my mother's headstone where

the wild peony with its pale-brushed lips

closes on the fiddleback.

As I look up, sky lanterns float,

and stars are strung

with angel hair hanging

in silk-white clouds

against thin air.

THE GIFT

For Gerald Stern

> *The world is but canvas to our imaginations.*
> —Henry David Thoreau

I made you a poem packed with galaxies
out of map-green tint from the nettle tree—

swaddled in bark of birch silky scent,
twined in spirals with milk-white parchment.

I stitched in bright berries from holly
the high-pitched qui-qui of brown coqui,

wove diaphanous shells of cicadas
falling chimes of rain from La Paz,

robed it with flossy ribbons
of peony petals and phlox.

Another world of other worlds I place
on your doorstep in the evening's haze.

Quietly. Listen past the music against
the scented page—Let it whisper.

PAISLEY SHAWL

        side   other   the   on Him meet I When

shine the from eyes my cover   and   shoes my off take   will   I

fall downweepingforjoyandcaress   His nail scarred feet   then

shawl paisley my in   her wrap and hands her kiss mother my find will I

TWO

ORANGE LANTERN. BLUE MOON RISING

enters the broken-horizon. A gaggle
of moon-gazers standing on boardwalk

benches stretch as if they recognize
family in the face of the moon.

Sky stabbed with light. Like star-jumping or like words
blazing from the deep pockets of the poet.

A certain kind of dazzle; snug like stepping
into wool slippers on Sunday morning.

PORTRAIT IN THE TREES

At the costume party in the mansion, I was talking to trees.
In the foyer, redwoods, beech, evergreens, and bamboo
jabbered—while carrying a banyan's tangled roots through
the French-Baroque doors, I gulped the still air.

Swigging a martini, a hemlock swayed under its curled
branches. Another spooned caviar, worked her limbs
like an aerobics instructor wrestling time. Showy leaves like
silver dollars flickered from the ocean breeze. In the parlour

a ruby-masked birch avoided eye-contact. I disguised
my yawning. The party heated. Discourse wafted up the
twisting staircase, nettle trees crowded the stone fireplace. Some
admired the classic gilt wall-panels, some multi-tasked answering

iPhones, some googled. In pearl bandanna & gold leaf
ensemble, the hostess gloated bloodshot rings, trunk peeling
from a costume malfunction. Swathed in spores & spider
webs, young willows slumped on the red-velvet silk cut couch.

Rolled cocktail napkins shot like game-balls across the marble
floor. Imported wine in Baccarat—
flowed like buckets of rain water, glasses of milk and honey.
The band played oldies—

trees danced like lemurs, puffed weed, sparks flew. Trees
squeezed one another, bragged trips & money, chatter like sticky
resin. Couples slow-danced the Sienna ballroom floor to
"Oh, I wish I had a river I could skate away on."

In the morning on the other side of the river, I toast health to the trees,
health to the wide-plumed creatures passing there, health to
the wilderness, health to the self needing to be explored. Health
to the poetry that comes out of this wilderness.

AROMA IN FLORAL

The poet is live
wood on the flowering vine—
the poems, muscat grapes.

THE BLESSING

> *Poetry is a momentary stay against confusion.*
> —Robert Frost

Neighbors say, *She's one of the three
Graces in ebony penny loafers.* Her wavy
stride, birdy body and nose.

Slender in blue jeans,
white hair drapes her shoulder blades
like a sun catcher washed

with light. Garage door rises 6 a.m.—
she's ninety, supposed to hobble,
moves like a schoolgirl ready for recess.

Cool September day, woolly hat,
scarf waves from her thin neck
like a spinnaker,

and she hurries down the wrinkled
driveway to tell her secret to the trees,
clutching a brown paper bag

walks toward her cement steps,
faces the greenest uncut lawn,
the drama of cicadamania,

mockingbirds, robins, the walled garden,
sweetness of sun, sky, woods—
the sweet, sweet, of being alive.

Carries the bag bursting
with bread crumbs—raises her hands &
flings with an otherworldly stroke

all the scraps saved from
yesterday—breakfast, lunch, supper
shredded white bread, rye, pieces of muffins.

Dry crust, croutons, crackers—she tosses
to the indigo sky,
body stretching like a maestro.

I watch this scene from our front window.
It is the second spring, I whisper to myself,
bread hits the ground,

animal prattle rings the alarm,
a multitude of chipmunks,
a host of sparrows and squirrels.

PETITS FOURS

The Walk

    On Madison Avenue, the Yorkie
    with owner on the rhinestone leash—
    takes arthritic steps.

                                  Boardwalk Hall

                           Seabirds flash wingbeats
                        against the moon—rant like
                           teens at a rock concert.

At the Kaleidobar in the Catskills

    The kaleidoscope
    streaming like a wild peacock—
    eye-candy on quills.

                                        Looking Glass

                             Wonder captured on
                             the face of a child
                             —startles the poet.

THE PINK THREAD

Interlude coats the inside
of each glass atomizer. I still

breathe in mother's honey-scent
still breathe out her haunting grace.

I can remember her in love with
the art of oil painting, how she studied

the Delft vase bundled
with coral peonies, the royal

pink pomegranate, the India
pink water-polished stone.

In those days she'd tell me, "Keep
fashioning, keep planting, making."

She spoke in riddles.

In her kitchen her shell-pink
refrigerator. She drove a salmon

Oldsmobile, wore blush
dresses and purses that matched.

My mini-dachshund was outfitted
in pink collar and cherry sweater.

She'd lean in twirling my hair, "Dream
in pink, my daughter, push back

at the dark."

BEAR

Black bear on my deck
gorging on sunflower seeds
near the prayer garden—

I offer him granola bars. A cup
of coffee.

THE VISIT

The once-upon-a-time
new baby doll with brown button
eyes and curly chestnut poodle-cut,

grows bald with hair unglued. While
mother flips through *Ladies Home
Journal* in the dentist's office, we close

the door behind us. Dad holds my
hand, leads me down oak-lined
Main in Jersey City to Goodman's

Doll Hospital. Dr. Mahler unwraps
the pilled-fleece blanket. Operates.
Hours later—

three of us glide on snow
covered sidewalks. I sing
a lullaby. Father hums

the "Halleluiah Chorus" as
he presses a worn handkerchief
against his brow.

PEELING

It's the same dream night after night. A gritty kettle on the nightstand,
steaming orange tea leaves immersed in a pot. My father's mother and
I are peeling oranges. Grandmother sits like a Renoir model in her raw

silk blouse, luxuriant folds, draped in yards of charmeuse, liquid purple-
gold flowing skirt—moss green cushions at her back, her left wrist
rests on the couch near a bundle of violets. On the sideboard,

a Chinese bowl, chock-full of sweet oranges, a cameo pin frames her
neckline, the snow white lace collar, her strong features, her level eyes.
Holding a paring knife, she selects the bright beauty from the fruit bowl,

carves thick luminous skin, moving the knife longitudinally, cuts
perfect crescents — split citrus, flashing spray. Are they
mandarin? Are they bitter or blood orange? Valencia,

Berna, Belladonna? Carrying a mesh-bag of oranges, grandmother
grows younger, melts into a cafe on the Champ Elysées—
Fog lifts into orange-geometrics, baskets of fruit sink into cobblestone

streets of Paris. The orchard-city blinds traffic, schoolchildren, Parisian
street musicians. Toting brushes and palette, an artist sets up thirty
easels near the cathedral, paints citrine landscapes in different light.

Citrus trees tower into merlot-colored clouds. My grandmother, like a
city of gold, wrapped in oranges from neckline to waistline to hemline.
Grandmother begins peeling like wallpaper head to toe. Grandmother,

circular like the mandala in my sketchbook—
Grandmother, peeling like wallpaper from head to toe.

I TURNED AROUND

On the nine mile hike
on the slope of Overlook Mountain—
He breathed into my nostrils.

AWAKENINGS

There are visions that keep me from sleeping,
my parrot, fishes, and ferret,
a new job, the skirt and blouse I forgot to iron,
thoughts of the alarm set for six a.m.,

mussels soaked in garlic that repeat,
the empty bottle of cab, head pounding,
the pot of Starbucks I drank at dinner,
accumulated emails I intend to send.

Noises keep me awake—
Jellicles in the woods yowl, the thump
of the cat on the bed, the on-again-off-
again ambulance siren,

and events—
an old lover crawling into my dream wearing
a kilt and carrying bagpipes. Even while step-dancing,
he circles the space plays *Amazing Grace*.

There is throat-clearing as I raise questions. Then he disappears.

I disappear into a fetal position—
the feline behind the wheel of my runaway
Masserati with missing door
startles new REMs
in black & blue technicolor.

IT WAS A DAY

    just like this
    mid   spring
          magnolias exalting
    the dogwoods,
    dogwoods exalting
    the sun

    The air was still   just like this
    The birds   kibitzing
    in late afternoon

    Have you ever felt
          immersed
    in eternity?

    My eyes
    were   bluer
    just like this

    The yellow   of
    forsythia
          and daffodils
    changed   my heart

    It is Easter 1982
    my pink chiffon
    floats   into
    wisteria

SEELEY'S POND

The reticent moon—

still the pond croaks in one voice

beneath the lure of the stars.

Luminous sun rising—

the frog-pool hushed like rose-glass

against green canvas—

I fold into the fluorescent earth.

EVENING IN JULY

For a moment—

a firefly distracts until

the smudged moon eclipses.

OLIVE AND FIG

From Persian rugs—
olive trees and tapestries,
blue herons, and chickadees,

from the sea—
a large room a long dance
I am from the lyric poem
—unwritten,

from the azalea & the robin &
bumblebee, the towering black walnut
and dogwood tree,

lavender fields—
the angular sky
magnolia's breeze.

I am from *Children should be seen
and not heard* or *Lick the Plate
Clean Club and you'll earn a quarter.*

I am from the planet of pomegranates
and fig trees, Anatolia blind country,
handfuls of pistachios & hazelnuts

befitting an Armenian queen.
From watermelon fields, the clatter of dice
against my father's backgammon set.

Flatbread & yogurt & string cheese,
a black and white photo
of *starving Armenians.*

Under my bed I gather scraps like
a bower bird. A striped hatbox of pale
seashells & dried starfish.

THE ANOINTED COW

Last night, my daughter made it perfectly clear, she does not want my mother's silver candlesticks, my Wild Strawberry Wedgewood, not my antique Delftware, the Waterford crystal setting for twenty-four, nor my great aunt's embroidered table linens.

She does not want my 24 karat charm bracelet with its miniature White House, gold music box that plays Moon River, not the Eiffel Tower, nor the porcelain Christmas tree, glass slipper, mortar board, nor does she desire the folded one dollar bill charm.

Lounging on her mid-century-modern white leather couch, she tells it clear as diamonds, she does not want her personally crafted electrified 3 story doll's house, with etched paintings, chandeliers, sofas, and built in book cases, with later added bar stools.

She makes it obvious she does not want the Dutch Master's painting displayed in our dining room above the sideboard, the one of the couple sitting in a dark kitchen except for the slant of light highlighting pears, the fruit bowl on the table, checkered cloth.

As my daughter reaches for her Crate & Barrel Napa wine glass, the one relic she claims she wants, in a low pitched voice, is the Victorian standing sterling butter tub with the carved cow figurine handle on the cover, the one where the cow looks unassuming,

her hind knee bent casually, her hoof about to stomp. The one where the inner glass vessel rests securely above the ice, the twisted knife balances between the prongs, and gargoyles, tiny creatures with tarnished feet, haul their load into the next century.

THREE

MESSENGERS

The world is a world
of another inside another,
each swells with water,

swells with stars, planets, galaxies—
kingdoms never clear
to the human eye.

I remember a time when
you and I would lie in the grass
and trace cloud formations

that moved across like a camera lens—
profile of a tiger, an ancient temple,
a church steeple, lady in a Hollywood hat,

polished stone, bowl of pudding.
Another world of clouds spoke
to us through stillness,

so different, counter to the map-green
ocean with its coral reefs & colorful fishes.
What relief we felt, set apart

from the weary material world.
We played games naming the clouds
and sought ourselves in their shapes—

heard ourselves in their silences
as if they hummed a song
only you and I could interpret.

THE EASEL

My father paints the world on his easel,
planted in sand due east from Down the Beach.
Like a thumbprint he colors the bezeled sky
in stars swirled-blue crystals, the sea in

chiaroscuro charcoal. Gives me
a painted shell, presses it to my ear.
I pass him a turkey sandwich wrapped
in waxed paper & a glass of Grigio.

A straight-backed wing chair
with pin-striped awning overhang,
I wait with him all night for day. His copper skin
like a brass kettle—he paints the canvas
in peacock feathers.

Notice how his brush flourishes
against mid-air, a king lifting the royal staff.
A terry-cloth towel, an imperial robe. Calls me by name,
directs his tenor against the horizon like Placido Domingo.

Wild watercolors. My father regulates
the citrine-moon, the tides. The white-breath
clip-clopping waves, collage of pistachio seaweed,
starfish frosted with dust. Water-polished
conch, the rush of the sea. The tilted
sky.

AT THE BEACH

    Sandpipers at their *mesa de trabajo*
       move like a machine
    cutting cloth on a diagonal line

    With each unsettling fold—
       they lift up in unison
    as a new foreman takes the lead

    Then return to their work-table
       feeding like sewing machines—
      Tututu Tututu Tututu

AMUSEMENT PARK

As the lights go out
on the Boomerang Roller
Coaster ride—
steamy air hangs
like a bank of clouds
an endless ghost ride,
fast pass house of horrors

my hands claw the safety bar
knuckles pale,
flesh drained of color

an odyssey of
swerves, curves,
jolts, drops
chops, whiplash—
sweaty palms, pulse-stopping
corkscrew turns, breaks that screech.

My heart skips after the first inversion,
we slowly climb tracks
as high as a tower of giraffes
lifts then drops me
stomach suspended 10 feet down.

Blow the shofar—
as I step out of my capsule
legs splayed on the rubber platform
my face pasty as sifted-wet flour
I look back, wobble and sway.

All of nature screams—
in some way,
we each live
our own hell—
just the details are different.

But tell me—
in the middle of the test,
what is in your gratitude box?
What is your claim to heaven?

THE CAT UNDERGOES A BREAKTHROUGH

Squeamish Jellicle—
afraid of stargazer-lilies,
afraid of the falling maple leaf,
the doorbell ring.

Just today, I noticed a change
in her walk. Tail perpendicular,
nose held high. Spindle-walks windowsills,
plucks tuna chunks from the counter.

Now I can touch her
—even kiss her tabby forehead.
Chases a plastic Pepsi-top:
swings the room like a toddler.

Swats the makeshift toy
thinking a mouse—

She rolls around the room
like a hula-hoop.
Acrobatic lucky cat
—a normal kid again.

AFTER THE SQUALL

I dig into my tote,
a flurry of winter finches—
their voices disjointed.

THE PALACE

    The smell of lamb
    roasting in her old house,

    the tired oak tree in the backyard
    aching from so many ice storms,
    branches covered in crystal ornaments,

    and the fleur-de-lis design she loved, scattered
    like gold-dust on her apron, handkerchiefs,
    wallpaper, pillows, switch plates, like the crest

    above the hanging framed watercolor of her
    private country palace near Paris,
    thousands of miles away.

    My grandmother had long fingers
    like a pianist. Worked hard—
    stuffing peppers, threading kabobs,

    layering pastries, braiding bread into
    dainty loaves. Plucked chickens and
    seasoned the lamb.

    Porcelain dinner plates, a red & white
    French pattern, toile with a rural scene
    of boy and girl, horse & cart & apples.

    She'd open the purple tin box
    of dominoes, place pieces on the table.
    I carried the game-box to the nursing

    home, brought her pears & we
    peeled oranges together. She asked me
    if she was still beautiful.

ODES AND ELEGIES

Desk crowded and not,

words dusted into being—

spring house cleaning.

DELILAH

Handfuls of hair. Drain clogged.

Clean your dreadlocks from the basin—

Do I look like your everyday Philistine maid?

Staring into the mirror, the clink of
thirty pieces of silver. Recapitulates.

WHEN THE DINER CLOSES

The patron in the striped shirt—
who fires names at everyone in
the diner, —is wasted.

Dull blonde curls hang across
her pale brow. Her houndstooth skirt, twisted.
On the ruffled collar, a smudge of lipstick.

She mumbles something at two customers
about how she prefers sarsaparilla
to expeller pressed carrot juice.

And then out of nowhere,
"What does it matter if you swallow
beer from Baccarat or sip wine
from a Dixie cup?" she hollers as
she raises her brow at me.

Spinning on her stool,
like a swirl of red leather,
calls her husband from across the formica counter:

"Hey, dum-dum, pass the sugar. Hey dum-dum,
you forgot to stir my coffee."

After I leave the restaurant,
walk the streets of Montclair to find my car,
I think of foods I despise—

spray cheese, liver & lima beans,
red velvet cake, corn dogs & heavy cream—
I make a face at the mirror in the store window:
cow's blood, anchovies, oysters, & black pudding.

Still back at the diner. How I sweepcrumbsontomyplate,
leave the tip under the salt-shaker and pay the bill.
Glance over at the gentleman in the gray shaded suit—
and the one last stale donut on the milk-glass pedestal.

SAMSON CALLS OUT

The scent of jasmine on his chest
his soiled hooligan heart

Touch my wounds—

spit on their fish-god, Oh Yahweh

TREE-WHISPERER

Trees whisper among

themselves in the evening breeze—

my blanket-covering.

FLIGHT

I imagine my grandfather sitting
in the living room of his house
trying to please his wife, in the bedroom
sipping tea, nervously pulling knots from silk scarves,

trying to please his mother who threw dishes
then stormed upstairs and refused to talk,
worrying about his two young sons and how
to make his getaway.

Mary his widowed mother dressed in black,
stern face, thin lips, squinting eyes,
uprooted from Diyarbekir, Turkey, escaped
the genocide wearing the clothes on her back,

came to America to live with him, her beloved son,
makes the argument against her daughter-in-law,
She is not the one I picked to be your wife—
makes the argument against his America,

his tailored suits, his striped ties,
his polished shoes, even his handsome face.

The story goes he marched downtown
one October morning in 1918
and bought three tickets.

In the middle of the night,
kidnapped his own boys,
held their hands and
caught the train to Fresno.

I CRY OUT TO DADDY, ABBA

How will I know the way—

Oh, Lord of my soul,

you who made me,

quiet my divided

heart and lower the volume

of the world-drum—

so I can feel you

breathing.

THE STORM

January snow: an albino deer
—walking on water, the sky's
slow opening. Down blanket
tucked under clouds spills
from the ashen sky.
Pipes of wind against stillness.
Beneath my boots at night
the crush of January snow.
At my back—sharp click
of the clock.

THE OLD MAN LOOKS AT THE GREENHOUSE FROM HIS BEDROOM WINDOW

Memory is the scribe of the soul.
—Aristotle

The gardenia plant with youthful buds in spring

In the summer, the gardenia flowering lush-white perfume in green whorls

When I look out the window in January, I remember to remember.

FOUR

WORLD WITH NO END

Inside the brand-new image
there's an old metaphor.
Inside the metaphor

is me.
Inside me
my psalm,

inside my psalm
an image.
Inside the image

a metaphor,
inside it
me.

Inside the new planetarium
there's an old chapel.
Inside the chapel

is me.
Inside me
my heart-stream,

inside my heart-stream
a chapel.
Inside the chapel

a planetarium,
inside it
me.

SHE HAD A USE FOR EVERYTHING

She would re-gift trinkets—
I had to settle for a wild cat from Istanbul
though I had no relationship with this porcelain cat.

It sat on her windowsill
with no expression. She would find a use for it,
tapping it with her ring,

drunk cat wanting to sleep. Grandmother filled its belly
with arak and slowly sipped—told tales of their escape
from the Turkish killing fields of 1915.

UNDER THE BEECH TREE

A piercing sound rattled my ear. The wind
blew through trees. I peered into the woods,
the forest froze for a moment

like hands on a broken clock.
An alien utterance, part shriek part scream,
my eyes fixed on a quickened-shadow,
a few berries and acorns scattered—

A blue object wrestled to the ground.
Inching closer I noticed the lifeless clump,
the crackle of leaves beneath my feet,
an invisible critter whisked into the pachysandra covering—

From the bough of the beech tree,
the forest watchdog called *thief, thief, thief.*

Like a torn piece of denim, the dead bird lay there,
plucked feathers glorious in the sun. Purple crest, ripples on wings.
Her strong bill, the color of charcoal.

Birds circled the battle site. The one on the branch
ranted a few more times and flew away. Even years later

I never tell anyone what I know,
how it feels to be stripped and plucked.

OH, IF I WERE A BIRD AND COULD FLY AWAY

What will you carry
to the other side—

a scratched gold cross
a package of saltines

the parka that covers you
as you bike across Europe
as you escape the ovens—

What will you carry
when death corners you,
unbuttons your soul.

What will you carry?

DEAR WHITE STAR LINE

gold leaf monogrammed china, puckered teddy bear; dear spoons, coffee cups; dear cathedral of barnacles, seaweed-wrapped doll; maiden voyage; dear broken chandelier; floating staircase, rocking chairs, dear noise like colliding trains; *He maketh me to lie*

down; dear Iceberg Alley; dear bow sliced like a pomegranate; immigrants below; John Astor, his mahogany suite above; dear Mrs. Straus; dear ship builder; dear Captain Smith and moonless sky; sacred starship, floodgate like the rush of alabaster horses; *Ye though I walk*

through collapsed crow's nest & bridge; dear choreographer; musicians' last call, icy-calm waters, dear grandmother; dear life boats, *peace like a river;* dear crackerjacks, polished stones, curtain of coal; dear lost prize; closed book, scribbled postcard; dear

unsinkable watertight; *For thou art with me;* dear 2:20 a.m., April 15, 1912; dearest

Queen of Hearts.

EARLY THIS MORNING

at Starbuck's, I thought I saw you drive away in a red convertible, top down. Later, the man chatting with the teller could be your double, hairy arms and smooth hands. The gentleman buying roses in the supermarket wore a boyish grin just like yours. Near the willows where we used to bike, a man slow-walked with his lover, arms wrapped around her shoulders. As I stepped past the diner and looked in, there was a familiar face at the counter. I knocked on the window. Patrons turned around & cheered—

I thought it was a sign, or a coincidence, or nothing.

THEY BE MORTALS

and yet they strut across Times Square
making melody, like two sirens, "Take a picture with us,
come on nothing to lose. We'll even paint your body

if you can wait ten minutes." Sculpted bodies, cheeks tattooed
with chalk-white stars. Both women wearing thongs,
one in striped bikini top, one an American bustier,

Old Glory, the only containment of their flesh.

Several years earlier, I imagine another,
a June day—sparkling sisters in spangled

summer dresses near the
duck pond with their mother.

THE WINDOW

Like a window that was once intact and
becomes shattered—
that is how I unexpectedly found myself in mid-life.
Now there's no misery: I've grown used to the
freeze. In the same way,
embers from the outdoor fire
no longer burn my eyes.

One day life's whole, incandescent, a polished
stone lifted to the light. Cloudless
like the spotless-surface of a mirror.

It was like that. And the next thing, a golf ball, flying from the 18th tee
with merciless trajectory, cracks the brittle wind, air currents vectoring,
frozen clouds splintering—and though you see it
hook sideways out of the corner of your eye.
It was like that.

Just at that moment, as you recline on the deck, a glass
of ruby-sangria in hand, stirring the fruit, licking your fingers
or perhaps you sip a cherry martini straight up, just before
you spear the maraschino—it was like that.

No time to move your house
down the road
—and it leaves a hole the size of a missile
in your bedroom window.

THE LIBERATOR

For many days now the world has been growing emptier.
For many days now my grieving body refuses to move,
food has lost its color, my beloveds are like bees
disappearing from the hive.

All night long, I turn like a flapjack
on a skillet until today I'm awakened:
The birds are back—birdsong, a storm
outside the window of my bedroom tower.

Even the cool alien air has a mint-note breath.
Can you ever have too much song?
Even the thin line of light squeezes past clouds.
Can you ever have too much light?

And how the Buchenwald prisoners must have heard
that same birdsong from inside the camp.
Day after day
I can't help thinking about that TV documentary,
the liberator of Buchenwald, that April morning, 1945—
they must have heard his jeep with its lyrical hum approach.

The American reconnaissance officer, no more than 25,
accompanied by two chaplains in a small military vehicle—

I vomited three times when I saw the first
likeness of a man peer out the small hole fenced in with barbed wire,
And so I began cutting the steely cords—

the prisoner's haggard face covered with pus-filled sores,
head teeming with lice, inflamed bulging eyes, rotting teeth,
half-ghost—then more faces appeared through the opening.

The soldier vomited,
took several snorts of whisky

from the flask in his back pocket—
clipped and ripped and parted all the wires.

One after another after another,
like phantoms filing out in grave clothes,
the liberator shook stiff hands, *Yes, we are Americans*,
he hugged an old man, raised up a child from the rubble.

As I look up at the sky, as I look through the trees,
I think, they are extravagant, the songbirds—
the bobolinks, thrushes, and sparrows,
with their cadences of psalms. I will get
out of bed now. The birds are back.

UPON VIEWING MASACCIO'S CARRIATA DAL PARADISO TERRESTRE

Their contorted faces, bodies bare, her arm
reaches to cover her breasts, her left hand hides
the soft flesh below her belly—blessed

now unblessed—sugar in the corner of
her lips. Slumped shoulders, he cannot lift
his head. They make their regressive journey

through the diameter of a different country, cities
of the newborn, land of pink slips, swollen tooth,
burst appendix, garden of tumors, the fever of tsunami.

I see you both handcuffed to eternity.

AFTER RAVENSBRUCK: THE WOMAN FROM HOLLAND SPEAKS TO ME IN A DREAM

The dream is the liberation of the spirit.
—Sigmund Freud

Out of the coal-black
she moved toward me. She limped and was very old.
Wallpaper backdrop curled like rolled dollar bills.

"I traveled the world with
my story, false wall in my bedroom—
the rationed cards."

Waved her sister's locket in mid-air. Suddenly,
it hung about her own thin neck.

"There is no deep pit—yet
He is not deeper still," she nodded.

She held up a worn leather-bound book.

"Carried it into the barracks. Like a stolen scrap of bread.
The She Wolf of the SS—
Angels distracted her."

She took a deep breath. "Lice were our friends,
read *Psalms* one-match-at-a-time." She paused. Then
circled me. Her wrinkled hands cupped my hands—

Asked what I will do with the rest of my life.

I LIFT MY EYES

Bright lights diminish into darkness,
reflections of posters of Clifton & Howe
in the window glass of the cathedral of arts.
Empty book tables,

volumes of luminaries, sold out.
The gates of NJPAC padlocked on
this late autumn Sunday afternoon.
I dig my feet into the silences.

Angels abandon their posts—drift through parking lots
away from the brick city, slow to arrive home.
I dig my feet into the rich soil
of giving voices—

I love this earth with its pastries & plenitudes.
As I lift my eyes,
I dig my feet into
the kingdom of poetry—

where the tarmac turns to feathers
and stones to pearl.

EVE LOOKS TO THE PEAR TREE

Eyes bulge into my head
Lips drop inches below my nose
Nose is absorbed into my face

Lids shut—I only see dim,
apple-bite fires an electric sting
through my tongue to my toes—

the din of the squall terrifies
and cracks my bones.

Up in the pear tree—

the chisel-bill-woodpecker throws
off his red scarf and houndstooth cape.

MEMO

Memory of you—

a torn kite undulating

through the galaxies.

BIOGRAPHY OF THE PEAR

There are only ten minutes in the life of a pear when it is perfect to eat.
—Ralph Waldo Emerson

Chinese yellow pomegranate.
Caterpillar surprise. Syrup of
sugarland. Perry cider. Buddha
belly. Old world native. Goldens
ignored by Eve. Buttercream bells
in the garden, a refuge in the trees.
Patio containers. Shrubs. Homer's
gift from the gods. Hums. Pear
pickers and pear drops; finches
hideaway. Partridge in a sacred tree.
Photo essay in chartreuse & curled
stem. Fashion story of the arboretum.
Mark Twain's savored soufflé.
Spiced, stewed, pecans & crumbled
cheese. Pyriform. French wild produce.
Succulent. Organic. Deciduous
pearwood. Pome fruit. Overripe fruit,
crestfallen, dimpled, caked with bees.
Aphids and honeydew leaves. Russeting.
Oh, taste. Pyrus, born from seeds
of faith. Brother to the stone peach
and cherry. Cousin to quince and rose hips,
perfumed Duchesse. William's, Anjou,
Bartlett white flowers. He loves me.
Backstory to the orange orchard. Mother's
go-to dessert, childhood's diamonds.
Wisdom's sweetheart. Musicality
on the tongue. A bowl of violins.

CHERRY BLOSSOMS

Her wool cape and galoshes
piled on my front stoop—

Spring entered the yard
today wearing chiffon
—she was barefoot.

Her down-jacket
and satchel swung
across our wrought-iron
railing.

She rang our doorbell
just before noon
carrying bundles of dogwood—
her toes were painted petals.

The breeze loosened her ribbon-tendrils
against the mint air,
the sun perfumed her wrists.

By midday
my front steps
looked like a winter warehouse—

neighbors discarded
coats and hats and mittens,
everywhere—
displayed across the
lawn like a department store closet.

Spring, like a moving symphony, tilted
her head and flipped her long curls,
gesturing to the crowd of strangers—

from out of her trunk, cable-sweaters and
scarves, gloves, goggles, and booties,
pullovers, parkas, and leggings

—strung on trees then disappeared
into piles
of dead leaves.

UNLATCHING

Cheerily cheer up. Tut tut tut—

First thought: Robins everywhere
blanket the neighborhood like

cinnamon splashes on a Pollock
painting. Glossy light, bright-bright.
In trees in birdbath on feeder on

sidewalk, tapestry covered ground,
mythological birds with magical
eyes and heads that swivel.

Everywhere—love thy neighborhood,
crowd the neighborhood like crushed
jewels in paint. Soon they'll be eating

in my kitchen, and I'll be foraging
earthworms. Soon they'll be nesting
in my bed, and I, wingbeats across

an ultramarine sky—ssip, ssip. If I could
stay forever, I'd smell the stringy lilacs,
rub my feet into kaleidoscopic green.

Where robins wrestle worms as
spring's clock ticks-out. Even the buzz
of their wings is sweet. Brick-red robin,

my elegant jewel folded in blue-green holly,
polished by the sun. Restores every
summer, every spring, stabilizing—sure as

clouds burst the gray stitches of sky.
Cheerily cheer up. Tut tut tut—
Last thought: What I don't know is how this

chorister backpacked from Rio to Central Park.
I dream of her peregrinations across
the timeline of eternity.

But what I do know,
is that in the rainstorm, I follow her lead,
easy to step the next step. Oh, feathered

creature, your blood runs through my veins—
shutters and windows and cage doors swing open.

Acknowledgments

I wish to thank my writing community for their support and encouragement bestowed on me during this writing journey. Much love and gratitude to Alicia Ostriker and Anne Marie Macari for reading these poems so closely and for their insights and generous support. And I want to express my deepest thanks to Gerald Stern, Natalie Diaz, Gary Short, and Jane Mead who continued to challenge and inspire me. Many thanks to Sean Nevin, Ira Sadoff, Mihaela Moscaliuc, Michael Waters, Aracelis Girmay, Ellen Dore Watson, Judith Vollmer, Afaa Weaver, and Sarah Vap for their graciousness and wisdom. And heartfelt thanks to Maria Gillan, Laura Boss, Sondra Gash, for their encouragement and inspiration, and many many thanks to JPG, my best critic.

Acknowledgment is due, to the following publications, with warm thanks to the editors and publishers of the listed periodicals and anthologies, in which some of the poems in this collection appeared, some in earlier versions or with different titles: *Adanna*: "The Easel," 2016; *Bowman Greenhouse Anthology*: "The Gift," 2014; *Climate of Opinion*: "After Ravensbruck: The Woman from Holland Speaks to Me in a Dream," 2017; *The Crafty Poet II*: "Under the Beech Tree," 2016; *The Great Falls Poetry Anthology*: "The Contest," 2014; *Journal of New Jersey Poets*: "Amusement Park," 40th Anniversary, 2014; *LIPS*: "When the Diner Closes," vol. 44, 2015; *Paterson Literary Review*: "Flight," vol. 42, 2014, "The Liberator," vol. 43, 2015, "The Anointed Cow," vol. 44, 2016, "Peeling," 2017; *The Paulinskill Poetry Project: Voices from Here 2:* "First Day of School for the Teacher," and "World With No End," 2017; *The Stillwater Review*: "Paisley Shawl," vol. 4, 2014, "In the Morning," vol. 5, 2015.

Notes

"The Gift" was reprinted in *Meta-Land: Poets of the Palisades II* by Paul Nash (2016).

"Flight" won Editor's Choice in the 2014 Allen Ginsberg Poetry Contest and "The Liberator" and "The Anointed Cow" received honorable mention in the 2015, 2016, Allen Ginsberg Poetry Contest.

"Wounded Angel" was one of ten finalists in the 2016 *Tiferet* contest.

"After Ravensbruck: The Woman from Holland Speaks to Me in a Dream" was written in memory of Corrie ten Boom (1892–1983).

www.ingramcontent.com/pod-product-compliance
Lightning Source LLC
Chambersburg PA
CBHW071201090426
42736CB00012B/2406